DAN SEABORN

101 Ways to Improve at Dadhood!

Practical Ways For Fathers To Grow Up With Their Children.

Published by Wesleyan Publishing House
Indianapolis, Indiana 46250
Printed in the United States of America
ISBN 0-89827-148-7

101 Ways To Improve At Dadhood!

Practical Ways For Fathers To Grow Up With Their Children.

Dan Seaborn

INTRODUCTION:

Being a dad is in! From learning to spend quality time with their kids to spending more time on their knees, dads are "coming out of the closet" and accepting their responsibilities. The purpose of this book is to provide some practical ideas for growing in your relationship with your children. Some of the ideas will be fun, others will require a time of internal inspection.

Thanks for joining me in this movement to restore the joy and blessing of family life to our homes, our neighborhoods and our world.

1

Surprise Your Child At School

Prearrange a visit to your child's classroom at school. Take along some muffins or sprinkled doughnuts. The teacher will appreciate your active parenting involvement in the school and your child will feel special all day.

2

Name Your Rooms

Take your kids through the different rooms in your house and name each room. For example, if there's a room with a lot of light, call it the "sunshine" room. If there's one with lots of colors, maybe the "rainbow" room. From now on, call each room by it's unique name when you're wanting to meet there or referring to it in general. Maybe even begin it all by announcing there's a special project after dinner. Get enough posterboard and supplies to make a sign for each room. Let the kids put their personal touches on the signs. Enjoy their creativity. GO FOR IT!

3

Make a Movie

Typically, kids love to be on video. I've found they get even more excited when they get to do the taping. Plan a time when you are doing something special and surprise your kids by asking them to go along and video tape the action. Don't worry if they get you in the middle of the frame, just let them have fun. You might not win $10,000 on "America's Funniest Home Videos" but you'll definitely enjoy your time sharing a bowl of popcorn as you watch the video together.

4

Blow The Horn

One of the best family times we've experienced occurred by accident. You can experience it too. When you arrive home from work, blow the horn in the driveway to let the kids know you're there and let them run out to the car. Plop one of them in your lap and while keeping one finger on the steering wheel, let him drive the car into the garage. Be careful that the drive is clear and all kids are in a safe position before starting, but this can be a great time of hugs and kisses as you arrive home. All of you can then run inside and tell mom you've arrived home safely. They will love this . . . trust me!

5

Let Your Kids Share

On a day you're feeling brave and secure, ask your child to sit down with you and share some areas they believe you could improve as a parent. Be serious and appreciate their perspective. Although you may disagree, don't argue. If there's constructive criticism to be found, take advantage of it and grow.

6

Give Love Away

Teach your kids about sacrifice. Together talk about families that are special friends with your family. Make a unique card for them and include a little surprise in the envelope. Explain why we need to encourage others and why giving is better than receiving. Let it be a lesson learned early and developed so they might continue the process with their own families.

7

Plan Ahead

Invite your wife and the kids to meet you at a restaurant for dinner. On your way to the restaurant, stop by home and leave little cut-out footprints from the entrance of the house to their rooms. Have a little surprise for each person as they follow the footprints. The surprise can be simple, it will be the thought that counts. Dad — plan on an excellent evening.

8

Make a Tire Swing

Go to a local tire shop and ask if there are any old tires you can have. Often there is an old tractor tire they are discarding. Follow the diagram on this page and construct a great tire swing for the kids. Happy swinging!

Old Tire

Cut out!

9

Start "Mom"ent Time In Your Family

Occasionally shout out, "It's MOMent time!" This simply means it's time to run and give mom a hug. Pick days when you're sure she's on her last leg or just needs family love. After you've had MOMents two or three times a day for the first week, give her a recovery period from all the bruises, and then make it happen at least twice a week. It's our MOMent.

10

Role Reversal At Bedtime

Have the kids read you a story, get you a drink and tuck you in before turning off the light (ask them to leave the hallway light on). Cue them to say things like, "now it's time to be quiet and go to sleep." Be sure to get lots of hugs and kisses and when they try to leave the room think of another question. Show them what it's like to be the dad or mom, and be sure to "fall asleep" quickly so they'll learn from your example. (**IMPORTANT:** Don't really go to sleep until you've checked on them and you're certain they didn't go to bed with the cookie jar.)

Keep A Journal

Keep a journal of notes you write to the children about day-to-day activities. Save it for a special day like their wedding day or an eighteenth birthday party. This will make a very personal gift that your child will treasure forever. You can even pass on your beliefs as permanent reminders. It's never too late to begin this book. Start today.

12

Leave A Surprise

When you're scheduled to be out of town, leave little surprises for your family. Place notes in their pajama drawers or gifts under their pillows. Make it personal for each child. They'll think of you as they go to sleep that night. (Be sure to leave a surprise in your wife's pajamas. Be creative . . . I'll stop there!)

13

Make A Tent

On a Sunday afternoon, turn off the NFL and find a blanket or old quilt. Wedge one corner of the quilt in a door. Bring a couple chairs over and drape the blanket in such a way that it creates a tent. Have fun sneaking goodies from the refrigerator to the homemade tent. See how much junk food you can eat without mom finding out. Let mom in on your secret by loudly humming as you walk by her with the goodies. Finally, let her become a part of it, and laugh and hug as a family.

14

Make A Special Poster For Your Office Door

Let the kids pick out favorite pictures of themselves and create a posterboard filled with these pictures. Work together to make a collage that you can proudly display at work. Others will appreciate the personal touch they see in this work of art.

15

Accept Your Responsibility

God has blessed us as fathers with beautiful creations called children. Our responsibility is to love these children with His love. We must teach our children using His Word as a guideline. Live by the example of Christ by doing what is right and just. Genesis 18:19 says, "I have chosen him, so that he will direct his children and his household after him to keep the way of the Lord by doing what is right and just . . ."

16

Listen

One of the arts we have lost as parents is the ability to listen. Most of us have had to learn this the hard way. It's normal for a parent to make decisions without much input from the kids. Take time to listen to their perspective. When they say, "Dad . . . Dad . . . Dad," . . . LISTEN! Those "dads" won't ring forever in your ears. They are numbered and precious. Listen!

17

Laugh At Yourself

Too many times we dads feel we need to be perfect and can't laugh at ourselves. The next time you miss your exit and have traveled four hours the wrong way and an overnite stay is necessary . . . laugh. Give the family the opportunity to laugh and poke fun at you because of your silly mistake. It'll make the trip a lot easier. Be willing to see the humor . . . laugh at yourself.

18

Take A Peek At Nature

Pick a nice Saturday or Sunday afternoon and take time away from the routine to check out a local creek or stream. Flip over rocks and look for crayfish. Catch a minnow. If one of you falls in the water, just laugh about it. Those shoes can be dried and even the stains from the soil will wash out, but the memory will always remain. Talk about the smoothness of the rocks and the continuous water flow. See who can get the most skips out of a rock.

19

Share Your Memories

Take your kids back to the neighborhood where you grew up and talk about the memories you have of all those places. Show them the playground where you used to play and the sidewalks where you rode your bike. Remember, your kids don't picture you as a child until you tell them your childhood stories. This makes you seem so real, so normal.

20

Make A Bedtime Tape

My kids' favorite tape is one I've made about childhood memories I shared with a friend named Robert. After collecting several of these stories on paper, I recorded them on a tape. At night, after prayer time, I turn on the tape and let my kids go to sleep listening to crazy things I experienced as a child. This has been very comforting for my children. They go to sleep hearing my voice. Try it on your kids. It works!

21

Make A Surprise Gift For Mom

Without her knowing it, sneak into a back room with tape, paper, crayons and scissors, and work together to design a creative card to give to Mom. Call it your "just because we love you" card.

22

Take Your Child To Lunch

Show up at school just as your child enters the lunch room. Make sure you stop by the office and get approval, then surprise your child by inviting him to lunch at McDonalds. It will give him a thrill and all the other kids will think your son has the greatest dad in the world. When you're at lunch be sure to tell him how awesome he is and how you just wanted to spend a little time with him. Make it a time of affirmation.

23

Take Them To An Airport

Park as close as you legally can to the place where the airplanes and jets take off. Lay on your back in the grass and listen to the power of those engines. Talk about science, gravity, and anything else related to aerodynamics that makes you look smart. The key is to look smart!

24

Say "I'm Sorry"

When you mess up, be willing to admit it. Few dads can say they're sorry without defending themselves. No two words will make as big an impact as these do. You're not perfect, so admit it, and be willing to grow in this area. Maybe you need to say it right now . . . just do it.

25

Control Your Temper

We all know this is difficult to do, given the circumstances we often face in life. Make a rule and have an accountability partner to help you keep the rule. DON'T DISCIPLINE THE KIDS UNTIL YOU'VE DISCIPLINED YOURSELF. In other words, take a few quiet moments to think about the best way to properly discipline the kids. (I'm writing this one for me . . . you can use it if you'd like.)

26

Buy A Puppy

Want to see some thrilled kids? Go to the local pet store, kennel or humane society and just look at all those faces. After a good long search and deafening of the ears because of the yipping, choose from the assortment. Puppies have a way of winning a place in the hearts of the family, and they bring out some new characteristics in the kids. Experience it for yourself. OH GO AHEAD . . . they're only kids once!

Admire Refrigerator Art

Wayne Watson's song "Watercolor Ponies", has a great line that says, "little kids won't be little kids for long." If your kid has a work of art on the fridge or the wall, go grab his hand and walk up to the fridge and admire the character and creativity of it. Ask him if you can take it to the office and hang it up there. Make a big deal out of it. Think about it . . . don't you like it when you do something great and people ask you about it and say it's the best thing since sliced bread? Give your child that special feeling.

28

Sing Verses

Most kids can easily learn ten Bible verses. Pick out some well-known tunes and replace the lyrics with some favorite memory verses. There are many such tapes commercially available, but I believe it's more personal if you can create them with the kids. Let them pick out a song, you choose the verse, and see what you can do! Make sure you choose verses suitable for children, and be sure the kids understand what they mean. Sing-a-long now!

29

Have A Water Balloon Fight

Wait for a hot, sunny day and give each kid (including yourself) 10 balloons. The one soaked at the end of the fight is the winner. To make it more interesting, fill the balloons with Kool-Aid (or some other harmless liquid). If it's something that stains, make sure the clothing you wear is disposable. Mom will be appreciative. Pop one on your head for a finale.

About God's Truths

"Teach them to your children, talking about them when you sit at home and when you walk along the road, when you lie down and when you get up" (Deuteronomy 11:19).

31

Go To Their Ball Games

No matter what's on your calendar, go to your kids' ball games or special events. It is important for them to see you in the stands and to know that you are there supporting them. It will be meaningful when you can describe certain plays and affirm the play of your child. Your participation in their special events will encourage them, and they will be more likely to carry on that tradition when they're raising their own children.

32

Pray For Them

Have a list of the top five prayer needs for each member of your family. Pray for one kid on Monday, one on Tuesday, and so on. Tell your family members the day you specifically pray for them. Obviously, pray for or with your kids every day. At night take time to place your hand on them and thank God for the blessing they are in your life. They will long remember that hand and the peacefulness it brings. You can't replace the value of prayer.

33

Scratch Their Backs

Surprise your kids some night by going to their rooms as they go to sleep and ask them if you can scratch their backs and tell them a story as they go to sleep. Plan on a special time with the kids and be sure you aren't in a hurry. One of the stories you might share is the story of their birth. Tell how special it was when you first held them. Or maybe it's the uniqueness of their adoption that you want to share with them. Give them a soft hug and wish them a good night as you leave the room.

34
Make A Kite

All you need is a sheet of notebook paper, tape, string and two pieces of straw (hay). Place the straw (two pieces) in an X on the paper and allow the extra straw to hang off the bottom end of the paper. Tape the straw in place and tie the string to the center of the X. Go fly the kite. Make the necessary balancing adjustments. Fly the kite as high as possible then cut the string and try to find where it lands.

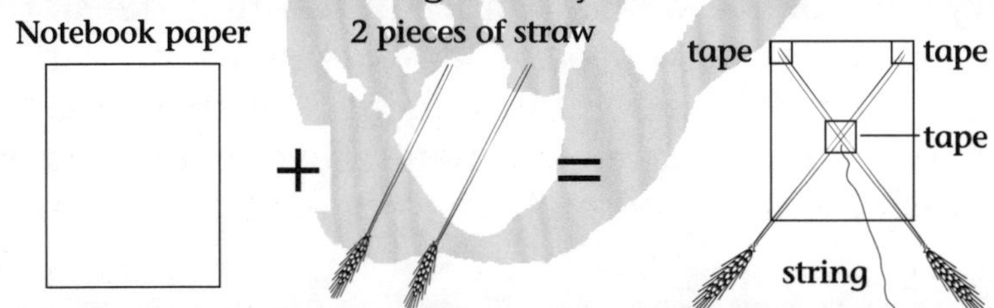

35

Ride Your Bikes To The Ice Cream Store

Preplan with mom a special bike ride after dinner to the ice cream parlor. Tell a story on the way about a time you got ice cream all over your face. Let the kids eat without napkins and plan on washing all the gook off later at home. Half the fun of being a kid is getting dirty. You can survive this one time, so go for it!

36

Give Them A Kiss

Make sure your kids know what it is to feel you softly kiss their face. Let them know how important it is for you to touch them. Let them learn appropriate behavior because of your example. Also, let them see you kiss their mom. This will be an important way to communicate her specialness to you. Don't go another day without it.

37

Invest In The Stock Market

A recent ad by Family Research Council in *The Wall Street Journal* pictured a dad rolling and tumbling on the floor with his kids. The caption under the picture said, "This dad's stock is soaring." This afternoon, watch your Dow Jones price soar as you spend that extra time investing in the kids.

38

Write A Note

Kids love to get mail. What a great way to emphasize your interest in them! Write them short letters, specially worded for their age, and see what fun and excitement mail time can bring. Be sure to include confetti to celebrate the moment. Volunteer to clean up the confetti to stay on mom's good side.

39

Take Your Kids Fishing

Here's a new twist: Go fishing in the front yard. Kids like to go fishing because they love to cast the rod and reel. Pretend your front yard is the lake, and see who can catch a shrub. Buy some gummy worms and bait the hooks like a pro.

40

Record A Message

A must with any answering machine is to let the kids leave the message. Help them be creative if needed, and let their voice greet any callers. Their voices are much more fun to listen to than yours. Such a message is sure to keep the caller from hanging up before the beep.

41

Go To The Dollar Store

Spend an hour looking for the perfect one dollar gift for each other. The most important thing you will spend together is time.

42

Ask Them To Paint

Recently I needed a table painted in the basement, so I prepped the room and floor and asked the kids if they would be willing to use the brushes and roller and paint it for me. They couldn't believe it. I even left the room and told them I'd be back to check on them later. Their ages are eight, five and three, but I was amazed at how great they did. Try it . . . you'll be surprised!

43

Have Compliment Wars

Every once in a while — at the dinner table or just playing around the house — call out the name of one of your kids and say, "(*Their name*), compliment war." Everyone else is to share compliments about that family member. Examples: She's a great kid. He is creative. She's fun to be with. He's a really good bike rider. On and on. The kids love it.

44

Create Sidewalk Art

Probably one of the most fun experiences I've had as a dad was when my three-year-old daughter asked me if I would lie down in the driveway and let her trace me. We had the best time together as she took a piece of sidewalk chalk and traced an outline of me. It was a beautiful day, and monarch butterflies were parading through the sky as I gazed upward. We talked about butterflies, God's creation and sidewalks. I will always cherish that day!! Try it with your kids!

45

Plant Some Flowers

Plant some flowers with the able assistance of your children. Dig the holes and let them drop the plants into their new home. You can pray for the Lord to add his blessing to their growth. You might even name a couple of the special plants for future reference . . . it might come in handy when you say, "Now boys, don't let the ball roll over Bert."

46

Visualize Your Tombstone

That's right, imagine your children standing over your tombstone. What will they say? What would they inscribe on it in honor of your life? Will they visit your grave often? Answer these real-life questions honestly and adjust some areas of your life if necessary.

47

Have An Accountability Partner

Let him ask you these 5 tough questions every week.

1. Have you specifically prayed for your children's needs every day this week?
2. Did you spend time with the children in a fun, happy environment?
3. Have you taught your children principles from God's Word this week?
4. Have you in any way jeopardized the solidity of your family this week?
5. Have you been truthful with me?

48

A Surprise Breakfast!

Get up before the rest of the family. Sneak out to the local donut shop and buy each family member's favorite. As they wake up, tell them you've prepared breakfast. Apologize and admit that you're not the best cook, but you've tried. WATCH THEIR EYES AS THEY NEAR THE TABLE AND THOSE HEALTHY, CHOCOLATE, SPRINKLED BEAUTIES COME INTO SIGHT. Get ready for a hug!

49

Play Checkers With Lifesavers!

If you jump your opponent, you get to eat their lifesaver. Be sure to save a few for crowning kings. Don't store the used game pieces . . .

50

Write A Poem

Write a poem to another family member. Let your kid help you come up with the main theme of the poem along with some rhyming words. Try to stay away from "Roses are red, violets are blue . . ." and similar well-known rhymes. Be creative.

51

Collect Cans And Bottles

Find 10 returnable cans or bottles and walk or ride to the store together. Get your $.50 or $1 and buy a pack of bubble gum to share. Split the whole pack, chew all the pieces and see who can blow the biggest bubble. Tell how you collected bottles as a kid and the "stuff" you bought with the money you made.

52

Jump A Ramp!

Build a ramp using a board and a tire. Place the board over the tire and teach your kid how to jump it on his or her bicycle. When you get brave enough, let your child jump the tire with you lying beside it. The neighborhood will come out to watch and it'll be the hit thing to do the next week. (Some parents are a bit leary about this one. You don't have to do it, but if you've got an aggressive one in the bunch, it'll go over great.)

53

Read Another Book

Just before tucking your kids in for the night, say, "You've been so good tonight I want to read you one more story." They'll be surprised — and happy — that you'd take time to read one more book without them even asking.

54

Ride Your Bikes To School

This will require a time of pre-planning, but it's worth the investment. Personally, I never rode my bike to school, so this was a new experience for me. It was great. We raced down the back stretch just before the school. We talked about the paths you could take to get there while keeping a watchful eye out for cars. Most importantly, I spent a time of laughter, racing and fun with the kids.

55

Go Camping

Go camping in the backyard. Let the kids help you pick out a great spot for pitching the tent. Take some marshmallows and other snacks to help satisfy those snack attacks. If you have access to a telescope, use it to view the stars and enjoy the beauty of God's creation. Psalm 147:4 states, "He determines the number of the stars and calls them each by name." Talk with your child about the awesome power of God to name and recall the name of each star. See how many you can name and remember. Relax in His creation.

56

Hug Your Spouse

Hug your spouse for 90 seconds in front of the kids. This daily routine will be great role modeling for the kids and will also build the physical intimacy between you and your spouse. How often do you hug your spouse for 90 seconds without other expectations? Good question!

57

Prepare Sunday Lunch

Prepare Sunday lunch for the family. Let your wife sit down and read the paper or enjoy a book while you prepare lunch. Ask the kids to help you set the table or put the ingredients together. Mom will love the background noise from the kitchen. Be sure to clean it all up while she takes a nap after lunch.

58

Go On A Missions Trip

The best way to teach our children to have a heart for missions is to experience missions. It might be as simple as helping serve dinner at the city mission or a more well-planned three or four day trip outside town. The involvement and hands-on experience they gain will be invaluable. Most of us are blessed to the point of being spoiled. Our children need to experience what the majority of the world faces on a daily basis.

59

Practice Colossians 3:21

"Fathers, do not embitter your children, or they will become discouraged."

60

Slay A Dragon

Talk with your children about a bad attitude or a bad habit. Tell them about how that small habit can become a dragon in their life that causes problems. Draw a picture of the dragon on paper and then put a big X through it to signify that you're ending its life. Pray together.

61

Pray "And" Prayers

As you pray together as a family, focus your prayers on a designated member of the family. Allow everyone in the family to pray a prayer of blessing or thanks, concluding the prayer with the word "and." At this point, another member of the family continues the prayer until the end.

62

Create A "Top Ten" List

Create a "top ten" list of the reasons you love your child. Share it with him at dinner time and hang it in his room or on his door. At night, be sure to point to one of the reasons just to affirm it in his life. This will not only build his self-esteem, it will remind you of the beautiful qualities of your child.

63

Back Off

It's difficult as a father to allow our children to battle through some of the experiences of life. Recently my nine-year-old son was threatened at school by a bully because he wouldn't allow him to cheat on a test. I immediately wanted to respond by teaching that kid a thing or two. As I sought the Lord for direction, He directed me to teach my son the importance of doing the right thing even when pressured to do wrong. I taught him the principle and allowed him to handle the circumstance on his own. It was tough, but it was right. Dads . . . let's learn to back off.

64

Practice Ephesians 6:4

"Fathers, do not exasperate your children; instead, bring them up in the training and instruction of the Lord."

65

Window Shop

In our fast-paced, no-time-to-stop-and-look world, many of us never enjoy a stroll past the store windows. Take your daughter for a stroll after a dinner date and enjoy talking about the odds and ends you see in the store fronts. Be sure to point out some of the beautiful qualities you see in her life.

66

Put Surprises Under Their Pillows

I often buy the boys a pack of basketball cards and sneak them under their pillows. After sharing our bedtime prayers I tell them to see if they have any surprises. They literally dive under their pillows to see what it is. Then it's great to open them slowly and read off the names of the ballplayers. They love it . . . so does dad!!!

67

Make A Billboard

Make a billboard and put it over the front door or in the front yard. You can vary what it says, but some good ideas are: AMERICA'S MOTHER OF THE WEEK! THE CHILD OF THE MONTH. WORLD'S GREATEST DAD!!! It makes for great conversations with the neighbors. Pass the billboard around the neighborhood and build unity.

68

Make A Candy Bar Poster

Make a candy bar poster for mom. Match different candy bars with words and give it to mom. For example: "Mom, you make me SNICKER. When I feel like ZERO you tell me I'm worth $100,000." (You get the idea.) The great reason to give it to mom is that she will share all the candy with you . . . dads won't.

69

Practice Proverbs 29:17

"Discipline your son, and he will give you peace; he will bring delight to your soul."

70

Watch For Teaching Opportunities

Many of the best times to share eternal principles with our children are when we're answering one of their 10,000 questions. Questions like, "Why did grandma die?" and "How do flowers grow?" shouldn't be answered haphazardly. This is a perfect time to pass on the trustworthy deeds of the Lord. Psalm 78:1-8 candidly explains how one generation is to teach the next generation. The verses that follow in this psalm are the tragic tale of what occurs in families where God's trustworthy truths are not passed on. Make the most of moments to teach for Christ . . . we are the teachers.

71

Remember What Kids Never Forget

Take time to make a list of the things you remember as a kid. Write down the things that mattered to you, the people who were your role models, the relationship you had with your parents. Make a list of the things you are doing now that will probably be remembered by your kids. Are you happy with the list? Are there adjustments you need to make?

72

Make Sure Your Kids Know Their Grandparents

It used to be that grandkids lived a mile or so from their grandparents. Families built houses in the same neighborhoods. Not so any more. In our transit society, grandparents are often far removed from the daily lives of their grandchildren. One way we can minimize the gap between our kids and their grandparents is by communication. A surprise phone call, note, or colored picture to grandma brightens everyone's day. Act now!

73

Set Goals

It's been written many times: If you don't know where you're going, you'll never get there. Set a goal for yourself and your family. Have specific educational and spiritual goals for your children. Keep those somewhere in front of you at work or at home. Read over them often and see if you are daily taking a step toward those goals.

74

Encourage Homework Habits

Moms often are left with the responsibility of being the homework enforcer because they're home with the kids or they arrive home before us dads. Too many times it becomes an area of conflict and can build frustration between mom and the kids. As a father, talk to your kids about their responsibility as students and how it prepares them for adult life. We are responsible to prepare them for the day they leave home. Homework is a matter of discipline. Enforce it!

75

Let Kids Be Kids

When I was a kid, I'd ride my bike for hours over worn paths around our house or jump ramps my friend and I had built. We chased butterflies and caught bumblebees in jars. I wore torn jeans and dad's old T-shirts. Now it seems our little tykes are off to baseball practice at the age of 6 and they've got to attend these four sport camps if they want to succeed and then they need to . . .
Enough already! Whatever happened to letting kids be kids without designer jackets and shoes? If your child wants to drop out of soccer to ride his bike . . . let him!

Put A Model Car Together

Here's a great project for Saturday afternoon. Buy a replica of a model you used to own and put it together with your child. Talk about what you did in the car and any fun experiences you can remember. Don't worry about a little too much glue here or a little spilled paint there. Enjoy the time . . . build a memory.

77

Hold Hands

When you're walking as a family, make sure you hold your hands out for your kids and wife. As you're driving, reach over and take the hand of your wife or kids. Too many men are afraid to show affection. It's important that our children see we are well-rounded individuals created in the image of God. To show sensitivity is a reflection of Him. Hold hands and stick together.

78

Read A Clean Joke Book

Our kids love to tell us jokes. Reverse it once. Get a good clean joke book and read it to your kids. They especially enjoy knock-knock jokes. Make some up if you want.

79

Practice
Deuteronomy 4:9-10

"Only be careful, and watch yourselves closely so that you do not forget the things your eyes have seen or let them slip from your heart as long as you live. Teach them to your children and to their children after them. . . . God said to Moses, 'Assemble the people before me to hear my words so they may learn to revere me as long as they live in the land and may teach them to their children.'"

80

Ask Your Kids To Pray

When you're facing a situation that's causing you stress, ask your kids to pray for you. Let them hold you as they pray. This will give them the opportunity to give back to you some of the continuous love you give to them. It also teaches them how to pray and shows them the power of prayer. Tell them later how their prayers were answered.

81

Test Drive A Car

This is one for the daring dads. Go to your local car dealership and let your son show you which car he thinks is the most awesome. Ask the salesman if you can take the beauty for a drive. Let your son turn on the radio and show him all the fancy gadgets. Have a great time just testing it out. Try not to get pulled into the salesman's office . . . that's trouble.

82

Cry

Only "real men" cry. Let your family know you're real. Jesus wept and so can we.

83

Laugh A Lot

How long has it been since you laughed so hard you couldn't get your breath? Were your kids there? They need to see us laugh. It brings healing to them as well as to us.

84

Stop And Smell The Toesies

This little piggy went to the market. This little piggy stayed home. This little piggy had roast beef. This little piggy had none. This little piggy cried wee, wee, wee, all the way home. If your kids are eight or under, this is still a great bedtime story. They will laugh as you pinch that last little toesie. When you've finished, smell your fingers and let out a yelp! Be young, act silly, have fun!!!

85

Date Mom

Once a week, or at least every other week, you ought to be out alone with mom. Tell the kids you're going out on a date. Teach them it is normal for a married couple to share romance and adventure together. Your children will see the emphasis and priority you place on the relationship with your spouse. Again . . . great role-modeling.

Practice Proverbs 22:6

"Train a child in the way he should go, and when he is old he will not turn from it."

87

Blue Plate Days

We've adopted this idea from Chuck Swindoll. On special days — and sometimes just for fun — serve dinner to one of your family members on a special blue plate. The plate signifies that you recognize that person as special, unique and wonderful to have in your family. It obviously should come out on birthdays and anniversaries, but occasionally bring it out just because . . .

88

Lose Sometimes

Whether it's Bingo, Monopoly, Checkers or one-on-one, allow your kids to beat you at their favorite games. Be a good sport and have a great attitude when you lose. Don't make it obvious, but do it! Competitive dads especially ought to practice this one.

89

Share A Popsicle

On one of the coldest days of the winter, drive to a quick mart store and purchase a jumbo popsicle. Then drive to a quiet spot with your child and turn the heater on full blast. Catch the drops of melting popsicle in your mouth and look at the funny colors of your tongue.

90

Build A Dollhouse With Cardboard Boxes

Just go to the grocery store and ask for five empty boxes. Cut and paste and paint and create a great dollhouse with your daughter. Pull your materials together over the course of the week, and book Saturday morning with her. Don't let anything except death cancel this appointment.

91

Take The Silliest Picture

Buy one of those disposable cameras and take pictures of the kids making silly faces or doing silly things. Have the pictures developed and let everyone vote on their favorite. Make a poster with the pictures and hang it up entitled, "AMERICA'S FAMILY OF THE MONTH".

Wash The Car . . . Together

Let your kids spray the hose and you do the rag work. Prepare yourself for a few drenchings, and be sure to dump a bucket of water over them. Be young, have fun . . . get soaked.

Take Another Child Along

The next time you're planning a trip to the zoo or the swimming pool, take another child along who doesn't often see families in a positive setting. Talk to your kids beforehand about being a positive influence and sometimes giving of themselves for the benefit of others. Teach love for your fellow man.

94

Practice Psalm 78:4-7

"... We will tell the next generation the praiseworthy deeds of the Lord, his power, and the wonders he has done.

He decreed statutes for Jacob and established the law in Israel, which he commanded our forefathers to teach their children, so the next generation would know them, even the children yet to be born, and they in turn would tell their children.

Then they would put their trust in God and would not forget his deeds but would keep his commands."

95

Squeeze Three Times

As you're sitting in an audience, while you're waiting in the doctor's office, wherever you find yourself waiting quietly . . . you can still communicate. Simply take your child's hand and squeeze three times and tell her that means "I love you." She can respond with four squeezes which means "I love you too!" My kids have done this to me while sitting in church or driving along in the car. It's a great way to show affection and love without ever speaking.

96

Have A Wobble Room

Do you and your children have a special place where you can go to work out a difference? Everytime we are involved in conflict situations with our children it is important to be willing to give a little and be understanding, a little wobble room if you will. Actually name a room in your house the "WOBBLE ROOM" and go there to resolve conflict. Be successful a few times and the room will gain a positive tradition in your family. Use it wisely!

97

Seek Presidency Of Your P.T.O.

You can have an incredible amount of involvement in the life of your kids if you are involved in this parent-teacher group. Your participation will make you more visible in the school, and your children will take notice! It's also a great way to influence your school for Christ.

98

Take A Vote

Plan a time when the family is going out for dinner, but don't plan where. As you get into the car, take a vote of the favorite place to go. (There's a good chance you could end up at McDonalds, so don't act disappointed.) Once the vote is taken and the verdict is reached, help everyone to understand the importance of being united in the decision. You can teach your children that life doesn't always work out the way we want it to, but we can go on.

99

Serve Your Children

Our humanity makes the word "serve" seem negative to us. Serving is actually a beautiful way of expressing our love for God. I want to serve my kids. I want them to know I can relate to their needs and desires. From board games to a game of one-on-one; from teaching to learning . . . I must be a servant.

100

A Piece Of Peace

The next time your family is in the middle of a debate, kneel. That's right. Kneel right in the middle of them and pray for God to give your family peace. If you need to confess . . . confess before your family and before Christ!

101

Start Over

When you've done all you know to do as a father . . . START OVER. Love again, smile again, laugh again, cry again, hug again, play again, write again, share again, date again, lose again . . . again and again and again . . . GOD BLESS!

Our Favorite Activities

#	Activity	Date	Comments
___	___	___	___
___	___	___	___
___	___	___	___
___	___	___	___
___	___	___	___
___	___	___	___
___	___	___	___

Our Favorite Activities

#	Activity	Date	Comments

I Corinthians 13

If I speak in the tongues of men and of angels, but have not love, I am only a resounding gong or a clanging cymbal. If I have the gift of prophecy and can fathom all mysteries and all knowledge, and if I have a faith that can move mountains, but have not love, I am nothing. If I give all I possess to the poor and surrender my body to the flames, but have not love, I gain nothing.

Love is patient, love is kind. It does not envy, it does not boast, it is not proud. It is not rude, it is not self-seeking, it is not easily angered, it keeps no record of wrongs. Love does not delight in evil but rejoices with the truth. It always protects, always trusts, always hopes, always perseveres.

Love never fails. But where there are prophecies, they will cease; where there are tongues, they will be stilled; where there is knowledge, it will pass away. For we know in part and we prophesy in part, but when perfection comes, the imperfect disappears. When I was a child, I talked like a child, I thought like a child, I reasoned like a child. When I became a man, I put childish ways behind me. Now we see but a poor reflection as in a mirror; then we shall see face to face. Now I know in part; then I shall know fully, even as I am fully known.

And now these three remain: faith, hope and love. But the greatest of these is love.

Psalm 127

Unless the LORD builds the house, its builders labor in vain.
Unless the LORD watches over the city, the watchmen stand guard in vain.

In vain you rise early and stay up late,
toiling for food to eat — for he grants sleep to those he loves.

Sons are a heritage from the LORD, children a reward from him.
Like arrows in the hands of a warrior are sons born in one's youth.

Blessed is the man whose quiver is full of them.
They will not be put to shame when they contend with their enemies in the gate.

Pastor Dan Seaborn founded Family Life Ministries, Inc. which is designed to give practical, biblical insight to families of all ages and stages of development. For more information or to purchase Family Life products such as shirts, bumper stickers and more, write Family Life Ministries, Inc., 130 Glendale, Holland, MI 49423.